Covered

Donora Hillard &
Zachary C. Bush

GOLD Wake Press

Boston, Ma

Theology of the Body
The Silence of Sickness
together as Covenant.

Theology of the Body
by Donora Hillard

The Silence of Sickness
By Zachary C. Bush

Theology of the Body

~~Donora Hillard~~

Donora Hillard

Diane ~ Hi! Thank you.
Hell is full of rabid
compositionists. ♡

Theology of the Body is defined as the study of how God is revealed through the human body; this is also part of Pope John Paul II's title for his collected lectures on the subject. It is being promoted throughout most Catholic institutions as a sexual counter-revolution.

If you have form'd a Circle to go into
Go into it yourself & see how you would do
~~ William Blake, *To God*

Thine eyes shall behold strange women, and thine heart shall utter perverse things.

Agape

Listen. You'll do what
you swore you would never.

Be nice to his other when
you see her, though she's in

AA with him and it kills
you that to survive he needs

it more than he needs you.
Don't say you hate her eyes.

Don't say you won't read
parts of the Bible because

of her name. Don't wince
when she says love can be

bought. Know you would
not for blood or God. Listen.

Instinct

I stroke the soft fur of my belly
as his eyes strip me clean.

Before, night blindness had
me scuttling along the ground.

Now, I place the sense of

his body beyond me. I see
him scratching his genitals

and sucking his fingers,
his stomach's center a lazy eye.

Werewolves

Howls wake me.
The moon like milk
through the window

in some warped film
we've rented of
gristle and wet fur,

canines descending
into pink flesh,
and him growling.

Creature

Stared at me under glass. Brought me home. Outfitted the cage
with a wheel, sawdust, a bottle that never dripped enough of you
into my mouth. Invited friends over to observe. Watched me groom
myself until the skin split. Took me to a field. Drove off.
You still find fur on your tongue.

She also lieth in wait as for prey, and increaseth the transgressors among men.

Pursuit

I have long fingers.
I'm taller than you think.
I eat red meat.

You can see muscles
in my legs from running
after men like you.

. . . we take into account the shorter and more violent curve of arousal in the man . . .

Remedy

My body wouldn't give
up its son that month,
my cervix a puckered star
he couldn't slip through.

Same for the clouds that
gathered at the waterfront,
heavy and gun-grey.
My husband watched them,

then offered to punch
me in the stomach
if the blood didn't come.
He called it a kindness.

It was customary in St. Paul's day for the bride to precede her wedding with a cleansing bath in preparation for her bridegroom.

Husband

I.
The lake has a woman's name.

On the drive to Perth, Ontario, the land like an old wound, his wife
told him of the dream.
In it, a woman bled onto a man's kitchen floor. One of her thighs
was raised.

I knew this woman was good, she said. He asked how.
She cleaned up after herself.

II.
He watches a couple go into the next cabin. The boy has a wolfish
face. The girl follows.
Their ring fingers are naked.

He thinks about how there are no great tragedies anymore. Instead,
people stumble into dark houses alone, catch hair and shreds of
dead skin in their throats.

He walks down to the water alone.

It is better to dwell in a corner of the housetop, than with a brawling woman in a wide house.

Rental

The heft of wet
clothing, catch of lint

in a trap. It's the first
season without him in

the house. The landlord's
door protests, wet leaves

lick my ankles. Tell him
this too will die.

Every woman, by virtue of the nuptial meaning of her body, is called in some way to be both a wife and a mother.

Wife

My husband was a shotgun made of candy.
I wanted to kill his former lovers, especially
the Strawberry Shortcake-looking one
who swore she was eighteen and the other
who scarred his forearms with knives he
later laid on my body. On our anniversary,
we made love in a kiddie pool full of sugar
and afterbirth. For my birthday, he blew
into fifteen pink balloons and set them loose
around the living room. Then he wanted me
to let his breath out and chase after them
with my mouth open, always wide open.

Mother

A woman suspected of cutting open a pregnant woman's uterus and stealing the infant was charged with homicide, unlawful restraint, and kidnapping, police said Sunday.

Police said the victim's body was bound at the wrists and ankles with duct tape. There were layers of duct tape and plastic covering much of her head. Her body was wrapped in a comforter and garbage bags and placed under the headboard of the bed in the master bedroom. She appeared to have been dead for about two days.

The victim "had a wound to the abdomen consistent with the removal of an infant," police said. "A very sharp instrument" was used to cut open her belly.

Authorities said the victim was 36 weeks pregnant. They were trying to determine whether she was alive when the infant was removed.

The suspect appeared at a hospital with a male infant that had the umbilical cord attached, police said. Tests later proved she was not the mother.

A decade earlier, the suspect was accused of stabbing a woman in an alleged plot to steal the woman's infant. A day after that stabbing, the suspect snatched a three-week-old female from a hospital after the child's 16-year-old mother had gone home for the night. The child was found unharmed at the suspect's home the next day.

The suspect then pleaded guilty to various charges from both incidents and got three to 10 years in prison, according to court records. She was paroled seven years later.

Adapted from an Associated Press article

Exhibition

The X-Lady was named for the X-like crossing of the straightened legs. The torso has been split open to allow the heart to be seen.

Two women walk together, hands clasped. One introduces the other to her mother.

Dissection of the head in this plastinate is unparalleled. The bones of the facial cranium have been opened like a book to both sides.

A woman seated at an adjacent table says, *Oh God, Oh God, Oh God* to no one.

Adapted from "Bodyworlds 2: List of Artifacts" (California Science Center)

Self-Portrait as Lines Overheard in a Bookstore

How about The World According to Mr. Rogers?

He asked me out once.

Stalker.

That's something I should have done, like, three or four years ago.

It's a sticky situation.

We put milk in it.

I didn't want him to

(gasp)

Stop.

I mean, I'm straight and everything.

The school . . . leads to the deformation of consciences. The development of young people is influenced by a distorted, individualistic concept of freedom.

Examination of Conscience

Have I been involved with magic?

Have I talked back?

Did I consent to passionate kisses?

Was I immodest in behavior?

Am I guilty of impurity with myself?

Have I written graffiti?

Did I reveal secrets?

Did I neglect to control my imagination?

Is my heart greedy?

Adapted from an inventory of questions distributed to Catholic secondary school students prior to reconciliation

The Profession

The stalking will
come; they are animals.
Remember you are
a hunter, the rifle alive
on your desk. Deliver
death from behind.
Shoot the artist first.

Adapted from John McPhee's *The Grizzly*

A Day

Directolordallouractionsbyyourholyinspirationandcarrythemonbyy
ourgraciousassistancesothateverywordandworkofoursmayalwaysbe
gininyouandthroughyoubehappilyendedamendirectolordallouractio
nsbyyourholyinspirationandcarrythemonbyyourgraciousassistances
othateverywordandworkofoursmayalwaysbegininyouandthroughyo
ubehappilyendedamendirectolordallouractionsbyyourholyinspiratio
nandcarrythemonbyyourgraciousassistancesothateverywordandwor
kofoursmayalwaysbegininyouandthroughyoubehappilyendedamend
irectolordallouractionsbyyourholyinspirationandcarrythemonbyyou
rgraciousassistancesothateverywordandworkofoursmayalwaysbegin
inyouandthroughyoubehappilyendedamendirectolordallouractionsb
yyourholyinspirationandcarrythemonbyyourgraciousassistancesoth
ateverywordandworkofoursmayalwaysbegininyouandthroughyoube
happilyendedamendirectolordallouractionsbyyourholyinspirationan
dcarrythemonbyyourgraciousassistancesothateverywordandworkof
oursmayalwaysbegininyouandthroughyoubehappilyendedamendire
ctolordallouractionsbyyourholyinspirationandcarrythemonbyyourg
raciousassistancesothateverywordandworkofoursmayalwaysbeginin
youandthroughyoubehappilyendedamendirectolordallouractionsby
yourholyinspirationandcarrythemonbyyourgraciousassistancesothat
everywordandworkofoursmayalwaysbegininyouandthroughyoubeh
appilyendedamendirectolordallouractionsbyyourholyinspirationand
carrythemonbyyourgraciousassistancesothateverywordandworkofo
ursmayalwaysbegininyouandthroughyoubehappilyendedamendirect
olordallouractionsbyyourholyinspirationandcarrythemonbyyourgra
ciousassistancesothateverywordandworkofoursmayalwaysbegininyo
uandthroughyoubehappilyendedamendirectolordallouractionsbyyo
urholyinspirationandcarrythemonbyyourgraciousassistancesothatev
erywordandworkofoursmayalwaysbegininyouandthroughyoubehap
pilyendedamendirectolordallouractionsbyyourholyinspirationandca
rrythemonbyyourgraciousassistancesothateverywordandworkofour
smayalwaysbegininyouandthroughyoubehappilyendedamendirectol
ordallouractionsbyyourholyinspirationandcarrythemonbyyourgraci
ousassistancesothateverywordandworkofoursmayalwaysbegininyou
andthroughyoubehappilyendedamendirectolordallouractionsbyyour
holyinspirationandcarrythemonbyyourgraciousassistancesothatever
ywordandworkofoursmayalwaysbegininyouandthroughyoubehappi
lyendedamendirectolordallouractionsbyyourholyinspirationandcarr

ythemonbyyourgraciousassistancesothateverywordandworkofours
mayalwaysbegininyouandthroughyoubehappilyendedamendirectolo
rdallouractionsbyyourholyinspirationandcarrythemonbyyourgracio
usassistancesothateverywordandworkofoursmayalwaysbegininyoua
ndthroughyoubehappilyendedamendirectolordallouractionsbyyour
holyinspirationandcarrythemonbyyourgraciousassistancesothatever
ywordandworkofoursmayalwaysbegininyouandthroughyoubehappi
lyendedamendirectolordallouractionsbyyourholyinspirationandcarr
ythemonbyyourgraciousassistancesothateverywordandworkofours
mayalwaysbegininyouandthroughyoubehappilyendedamendirectolo
rdallouractionsbyyourholyinspirationandcarrythemonbyyourgracio
usassistancesothateverywordandworkofoursmayalwaysbegininyoua
ndthroughyoubehappilyendedamendirectolordallouractionsbyyour
holyinspirationandcarrythemonbyyourgraciousassistancesothatever
ywordandworkofoursmayalwaysbegininyouandthroughyoubehappi
lyendedamendirectolordallouractionsbyyourholyinspirationandcarr
ythemonbyyourgraciousassistancesothateverywordandworkofours
mayalwaysbegininyouandthroughyoubehappilyendedamen

RELIGON

FAITH
God
Mom
Jesus
Dad
Lydia
Chairs
My Bed

BELIEF
<u>Holy Gost</u>
I belief in
Heaven + Earth
the forgivness of sins
and life in heaven
after we die
I do <u>not</u> believe in
purgarty.

Chorus from the Land of Grownups

She's stapled her plaid skirt shut. I want to ask who the glitter glue-
on nails I found under a desk belonged to, whose clot of blood it
was I smeared with my shoe in the restroom. I visited it days later.
It had dried and flaked, as if scratched with a fingernail.

There's a lesson in the cafeteria on how to sit. (*Don't straddle.*)
There's also a Student Council meeting about ways to get the boys
to stop chewing tobacco and jerking off in the lav between classes.
They've been writing on the walls with themselves.

. . . those who cannot exercise self-control . . . should marry . . .

Colleague

While rushing back to the man she lives with but is not married to,
she almost hits and kills a child riding a bicycle.

(*the young skull denting pavement, the cracked, slippery shell sliding
between her palms*)

After, she thinks of the boy who can say *pussy* and *thank you* in one
deadly sentence, a pearl of want in her throat.

Tutoring

The air hitches as the father lurches in. *Hi*, *Pop*, the boy says.
Pop slurs an *Is he behavin'*?, paws the fridge. The boy shrinks
sixteen years and six feet, six inches down to a doll's frame,
whispers *Sorry*. Forgive me for wanting to have birthed him
then. He must throw himself into this world of men, wailing.

Ruin

I am given articles written
by former priests who
warn of repeating mistakes.

They fear debt and dust,
rusted nails, and knuckle
cuts that keep opening.

They don't mention the
cracked miracle of seeing
just how bad it can get,

as when my students
watch footage of sports
injuries, sockets spinning

on hairpin turns, the bodies'
glittering calcium always
failing in the same place.

Most Accidents Occur Close to Home

The dean is to my left. He consults the ceiling, puffs his cheeks. His knees bounce as though he is cold. No one can control the temperature in this building. I look down at my hands. There is gore on my nails from shredding my lips, a nervous habit.

The principal is seated across from us. Her wardrobe has earned her the nickname Couch Killer. There are papers across her desk. Her glasses glint. *Students were heard discussing one of your poems*. She won't say which one or what students.

Both the superintendent and Catholic Identity Committee, who wrote an angry letter to the bishop about a novel since it was titled *The Patron Saint of Butterflies*, need to read it. My contract will not be renewed for next term, and I may be let go sooner.

Why couldn't you have written something nice. I don't answer. He was middle-aged, uncircumcised, and hairless. He bound my ankles and wrists together with twine. He clamped clothespins on my nipples and then raped me with a white candle.

The principal produces a tissue box in a sweeping gesture. They have nothing further. I see my boss in the hallway, her breasts pendulous. It is casual Friday. She sneers at me. *I just can't handle anything else this morning*, she says. *Not one more thing*.

I will prepare to leave here. I will sell my rings, Clorox my skin, avoid all collisions. There will be nothing left to mark my departure. No muscle, knucklebone, or glass eye. Nothing to cut out or pray for. I will soon forget the sound of their howling.

Summative

Areas to be addressed for the retention of the instructor:

1. *Students should remain quiet.*

2. *Students should stand to participate in the Pledge of Allegiance.*

3. *Students should remain seated.*

4. *Students should not be permitted to leave.*

5. *Every minute in the classroom should be directed toward engagement.*

6. *Be mindful of professional dress. Cover tattoos, scars.*

7. *Topics such as one's future plans should be kept to oneself.*

8. *Please expect all to behave in this manner.*

Indicate you have read this information and understand.

If we ever need to know how to properly love a woman, all we need to do is look at a crucifix.

Pillar

Carry me into your warm room.
I don't care if there are flying ants or that
you plan to kill yourself before you hit thirty.
You have warned me enough.
I came to you, one vein already open.
You bent your long, broad body in half,
kissed my wrist, drank to that.
We can become something, you breathed.

Thirty Seconds of Applause

Your hands in the mail today.

Yes, yes. All of this ether.

Your veins covering the page.

Apologies, I'm falling.

Your voice like rough water.

Plagiarist

I copied your name onto my forearm. I meant I wanted to accuse
rather than remind.

I meant I would have stolen your skin before you turned me into an
autistic teenager.

I meant men gave me their teeth before you came. I meant the ink
bled. Your name.

How to Love a Surrealist

Try to ignore poems he's written
for women before you comparing

their feet to lemons. Laugh when
he claims ants follow him everywhere.

If he doesn't call you one night,
picture him in Detroit, cutting his hair

in the mirror with kitchen scissors.
When he finally whispers *I love you*

for the first time, know he really means
The axe has hit the staircase.

For a whore is a deep ditch; and a strange woman is a narrow pit.

After *The Texas Chainsaw Massacre*

I.
So that you would love me,
I told you how I spat in the face
of the man who beat me for two years.
How I laughed, manic like the heroine,
even while he sank his teeth into my thigh.

II.
I thought of furniture made of bone.
A feather-covered killing floor.
The body's meat hoisted onto a hook.
How I wanted you to twist my will,
drag me into a room, and slam the door.

Wives, submit to your husbands as to the Lord. There is a sacred order to love. Isn't this what the knight-in-shining-armor romantic fantasy is all about?

Romance

My body is not
made of tiny violins.

It fails like your
Don't question my holy

need for your cunt anymore.
I watch your name

fall from my mouth.
Watch your mouth.

Watch my thighs
weep for you again.

The sexual revolution of the 20th century is simply inexplicable.

Theology of the Body

The freshman girl goes down
in liturgy. An ambulance whines.

The speaker says, *Ladies, your*
bodies don't make much sense

on their own, do they?
I hear other girls in

the restroom rasping to one
another, *It's just like being*

fingered with something metal.

In Michigan, you slit your wrist.

. . . we must be willing to die rather than ever indulge our lusts.

Devolution

Then it happens. We're no longer locked together with me calling
Sorry to the neighbors. Your ribs stop speaking. Your fingers slip
from my mouth. I cut my lips into ribbons and lick the loss.
You count the names of the dead.

So, many ask, will there be sex in heaven?

Winter, Michigan

you pinned me up against an oak in a park near where you were
young and your hand sang inside and you were the resurrection
you were violent light behind the mountain

Prayer

Praise you lest I never rest beside you in your city, seizing as ice falls. It will leave us bone-cold, a fractured reminder, and if I can't find words, know I tried, the event paralyzed, my tears running, freezing.

Lake St. Clair

There is a house. A bed and its implications. A man and woman unused to mercy. The old jokes: *Stay away. We're bad news.*

A kindling in the throat. Then water, metal.

There will be an oath made in blood, in hair. He will lay his knives down on her. She will talk to him with her whole body.

Given

Someone plunged a knife into a table

and said, *This is my body*.

If God is a lover chasing after his

beloved, your heart is an

altar, your face a cathedral window.

The Silence of Sickness

Zachary C. Bush

Finding Paradise

My skin cracks into
a thousand snake-scales

Blood-horny hyenas
scatter sideways
in every direction
like summer lightning
across the coal-grey plateau

I climb down from
my mountaintop
as it is safe now
on the backside

How This Man Breaks

The man hasn't left his bed for some years,
And he *still* won't; not for anyone, or anything.
It's as if he has completely lost track of time
Ever since his family abandoned him alone
In his home. Everything is silent.

❖❖❖

For weeks, before his wife left, the man listened to her snapping
Branches against the kitchen floor, until she had enough
To build the sled she slid down the street and out of his life.

Not too long after her departure, his children fled on ice skates,
Shredding through the front door they had left wide-open
From either forgetting, or not caring, their father remained inside.

Then the January winds burst through the gutted halls,
Spilling the cold moisture that soon solidified,
Until every inch of the man's house was frosted silvery-white.

❖❖❖

Balled-up in bed, Silence addresses the man directly,
And though he can't understand what's being communicated,
The man senses that he might already be dead. Frightened,
He tries to remember what his life was before it was not, but
There is nothing besides the blurred image of an exploding beehive.

The man buries his bearded face into the aged-yellow
Pillow. The sour stench of dry blood mixed with oils
And sweat scorches up his chaffed nostrils.
He whispers *I'm a shadow frozen to these sheets*.
Then he rolls over and shouts,
"Come back…set me on fire!"

Gazing Father

Some stars don't just fall and disappear,
And most don't explode all at once.
It's not that simple, it's not like all of the sudden
There's this cosmic Wop Pop-Pop BAM! No,
A star death takes time; explosions are a process.
It's like some stars are stronger than others. Maybe
There is a universal timeline, or maybe there is no order.
It's probably wrong to expect a star to glow forever,
Even if you swear your star is unique;
The process is impartial to favoritism.
So, as I put my sunglasses on,
I prepare myself for this final explosion,
The one that my unique star is 65 years ripe for. Yet,
No matter how much I hope for a different ending, I know that
Once it happens, there'll be no brilliant showers of golden dust;
Nothing will reach down to touch and comfort me.

WINTER PARK

Colorful snapshots spread across the fridge:
pink babies, sandcastles, piano recitals, weddings,
and smiles fade under pale streaks of yellow dust.
Morning sunlight spills through the window and slips
inside the liquor cabinet— stained glass patterns swirl.
The stench of syrah, sweat, and sickness drape the condo.
A bottle spins slowly on the countertop, and from its lip
wine streams over the edge, trickling onto the crown
of the old man wilted at the base of the cabinet.
Milky eyes bulge from his scotch tape skin.
And with veins wrapped around a glass, he tips the rim
against his purple puckered lips—a total darkness.

BLURRY FACES HOVER AROUND ME

and tongues slip through wrought-iron bars like oil-slick snakes,
prodding my ribcage; as I hang by a foot, in a birdcage, suspending
in slow spin.

"Because they assume the boy is the most sensitive member of the family they discourage him from spending time with them in the kitchen and by doing this it is their careful intention to not only protect him from himself but to also protect him from the sadness of the world..."

Just as a jaw works lips around a straw,
the silence sucks up everything
from behind the swinging kitchen door
still, the boy hides, eyeing through
a t-bone hole in the mahogany,
observing his present
family affair:

He scans what he can
of the kitchen, and the living
room where his eldest sister is smirking
and tugging rough on a black and curly
that's sprouted from the chin of his youngest sister
while she tries to swallow the last swollen *Froot
Loop* from a tipped bowl of rainbow-swirled milk.
There is a delay in her reaction—a shrill scream
and a speckle of blood—when the hair is ripped loose.

The boy sees his mama stretched flatback down the XL window-
sill where she sometimes monitors the movements of the sea. Yet
today, sea or no sea, she's transfixed beneath the strong technicolor
spell of her TV—silently shredding her emotions against the sharp
sparkle-garble of the Channel 4 Sunday Morning Minister, what
with all of his excessive hair gel and hallelujah dramatics! She's
shedding
tears that streak down the forever-gray of her sunken cheeks.

He then spots his twin going wild
in the far corner—pink face, with a sweat glaze,
swollen-over from the struggle to suppress the hoarse
moans of masturbating under the family dinner table
without anyone noticing and interrupting his pleasure,
or telling him not to disturb his not-quite-dead father,

who hasn't been himself in years. The aging man is
propped up awkwardly in his chair,
against the table, crumbling silently—*an infinite,
incurable silence*—like a discarded window mannequin.

Once through the backdoor of The Mansion of Sleep, we took a fantastic leap from the marble threshold and closed our eyes. There were colorful variations: Nebraska, Nebraska, Nebraska.

We landed in the middle of a wheat field. Bir-thing. Eyes open. An embryonic path snaked through all that endless wheat, dividing the red-rust stalks like opposing river banks. If, with your own eyes, you were to follow the path all of the way, then you'd see how it entered the jaws of the woods. Well, we saw, and, in an instant, we knew...

Those woods were *the* reason why we had fled The Mansion. Slip. There we would search for all that Sleep had stolen from us.

It was hot. There was an invisible decay. There were flies and unanswered questions.

We trudged the stick-pink, twisting trail. Overhead high-chirps and guttural echoes competed for the loudest echo. Beneath us fallen tree branches seemed to stretch on forever and across the ancient roots of trees; trees that were once great looming powers, but were now incomplete amputees.

It was then, in the woods, that we heard *them*—our abducted dreams—calling us by our first names from inside the branches at our feet. But as we reached down to snap and release them from the bark, we noticed the moonlight fading. There were no more shadows stretched across the forest floor.

We looked up to see the moon being eclipsed by a creeping canvas of blackbirds flapping across the sky. Our direction was lost. More questions. As we were sucked into the vortex of darkness—while overhead noises overwhelmed The Dream Talk and the birds smothered the moonlight—we realized that we had nothing to show that we'd gotten the better of Sleep. Skip. Breathe. Skip. Merriment. Be nauseous. There was nothing to prove that we had ever existed outside of The Mansion.

The Night He Was Committed

All night I heard lots of echoes, bleating
Like feral beasts, or a distant nightmare,
Maybe. Yet, the sounds were strong,
So strong that they overpowered the GONK-
GONK, GONK-GONK of my alarm clock
Trying to warn me not to open my eyes,
Not to roll over, and not to get out of bed;

But, it was useless. I couldn't even *begin*
To pretend to be still, and so I shuffled
Down the hallway, straight into the hourglass
Morning; which was blacker than black,
And devoid of my own delight in shadows.

As I moved in on the echoes, I heard them stretching
Purer as I neared our condo balcony, and that was when
I saw her on the other side of the sliding glass door. There
My mother was bowed into the bars, griping iron,
Her face was tangled under wild, long pepper-vine hair,
And she was screaming her years out to him. Then I knew
Her private attempts to shatter the silence of his sickness.

In the Shower

Your laugh penetrates through shadow walls, trading fragmented light for shards of porcelain plates— all those memories have been swept away, collected beneath warm blankets of convenient amnesia.

STRUCK

The man watches the silver sky shed
hundreds of doves over his land,
like unwanted babies tossed from tall buildings,
corkscrewing through the clouds, until brittle beaks
and bones break against the surface of the lake.

All Hunger is Silent

Morning's sky is colored with eleven shades of red light,
Leaking out from the lace of the lavender haze,
Staining all the dew of the treetops that border this stream
Where a boy sits, listening to the sounds of beavers' teeth
In construction upstream, gnawing through a soggy cypress trunk,
Until the crunching stops suddenly, and the slender tree topples
over, Slapping the belly of a dam. Waves ripple downstream.
Out of the corner of the boy's eye emerges a water moccasin. He
studies The snake's spin– an infinite circle on the ribbed surface of
the stream.

The Most Beautiful Thing I Have Ever Seen

Some homeless men come out the corner store
And walk to Jay's old empty car repair
A shop where metal scraps are sold by day
Where lost soul wino-junkies meet by night

The men are standing, shifting shoeless feet
While sucking bottles deep in paper bags

The youngest man walks away and spots
A rose that grows from cracks beneath his sole
He wraps his hand around the rose for warmth
Like flames that curl from cans in winter time

This is what went down before she turned me into stone...

High-noon sun filters through the bulky drapes, illuminating the motel room a rot-green. She reclines, naked and wet, in a red chair near the window. With a white towel wrapped around her head, her hair slithers down her long neck like black snakes, threatened. She spins a diamond ring on the table, taking deep drags off a Virginia Slim that teeters between her lips. She asks, "Did you think this would suffice?" The cigarette smoke curls up in thin spirals from the glass ashtray near her right hand, shaking. And the ring spins faster, blurring into a magnificent cloud, a hundred shades of silver.

ROYA

You turn sixty-five this year, and the silver sliver of an "L" fades from your signature.

Do you remember the night we first met?

E. hung off my shoulders, her warm breasts against my shirtless back. "Surprise Zachary," she giggled. You looked up at me from atop the cedar-wood desk, like a black cat, yellow eyes, cautious. You reeked of spoiled ink and musk. "Type something great while I prepare your birthday cake," she said, and left the room.

I named you ROYA, short for *Royal*, and referred to you as my black-iron battle tank. And like a tank, I drove you through the desert, each night, in search of images. It was only a matter of time before I was lost.

E. would ask me to stop typing and get back into bed, but once I started, my fingertips pelted your keys like summer hail. The rata-tat-tat ascended to something hypnotic, a spiritual symphony, like the church organ of my childhood. When I paused to load more paper or compose a thought, you would laugh. I wondered if it was not at me.

How many times have you locked your keys since she left?

I wish I could release the margins of guilt, just shift through time to when she and I were happy, and backspace over her tears with asterisks. But I chose you, and words stick.

Ink cannot be erased, leaving all my mistakes in front of me.

Our Home on 105-A W. Wayward Way

I see the red door where we welcomed evening,
Where you ripped every poem I wrote you.

I see the shelves where you left love notes for me,
Where you left your copy of the house key.

I see the white walls where we hung paintings,
Where you pinned me by the throat.

I see the rug where we tore into duct-taped boxes,
Where you stomped down on my bare foot.

I see the table where we watched Beta blow bubbles,
Where our metal forks scraped against plates.

I see the standing frames where our pictures were,
Where all our pictures had been plucked by you.

I see the desk where the surprise typewriter sat,
Where I lost myself in a world without you.

I see the shower were we prepared for the day,
Where we washed wrong words away.

I see the backyard where we carved pumpkins,
Where you cut your finger teaching me.

I see the porch where we hung cotton spider webs,
Where we stood in costume as Batman and Bumblebee.

I see the bed where I laughed at your spiritual requests,
Where you asked to hold my hand and say a prayer.

I see the washer where you emptied my jean pockets,
Where you left your cherry-print underwear.

I see the purple shards of porcelain where you threw a lamp,

Where it just missed hitting me.

I see the couch where we planned our future,
Where I told you I would no longer be a part of it.

When I heard the bear coming

my arms were filled with ten percent of everything I owned.
You cursed my name into a pillow, as I ran out our front
door.

The Winter Migration of Blue Crabs

E. never warned me.
E. never woke me.
I never heard them.

Whit, why are they in my head?
Unexpectedly queer.
I was asleep for a time, wasn't I?

E., she made this possible, didn't she?
The screen door was left ajar
after dinner. E. heard them,

the haunting tap dance
of a thousand crab claws
waltzing across the linoleum floor.

My bed is warmer than the kitchen.
In the winter, crabs seek warmth.
I don't blame them for this.

The crabs slipped through the cracked bedroom door
and scaled the sheets blanketing my head. They
popped my skull off like a bottle cap.

The night the blue crabs migrated to me,
I dreamt of acupuncture, a subconscious relief.
But still they poke at me and it hurts

E. why didn't you warn me?
E. why didn't you wake me?
I never heard them.

Disregard me

like ashes falling off the cigarette tip, she carelessly flicks,
while preparing her day. . .   .

In the Abandoned Hours of Morning

The sun was rising
Up over the pines
When I heard Amy
Screaming from inside
Her old man's farmhouse

From behind a bush
In my wooded yard
I watched a doctor
Step out their front door
His head hanging low
And when he let go
The knob was stained red

I ran to the side
Of the house to see
Through the cracked window
Red palm prints along
The hallway's white walls

Harvey was crying
Curled up in the corner
Ripping the stuffing
From the belly of
His daughter's rag doll

We Swallow(ed) Spiders in our Sleep

& honey on white tees attract ants
You look so peaceful tonight
While two cockroaches rest atop
Your eyelids shut, you are

Next to me, snoring
While I lust for
The other woman
I barely knew

You are loud in your sleep
Scaring the roaches
Down the bridge of
Your crooked nose

& I am alone
Remembering the morning
When we moved into this house
Gnats sucked the sweat
Shine from your legs
Until they had their fill

They drowned in you
I watched them, motionless
Freckle your creamy skin
I barely knew

[[[into this space]]]

I *am* slipping away_____

Where shadows run backwards
Screaming FIRE

That invisible light

Where moths suffocate
& shrivel by the thousands

At my feet

In the Hands of 1,000 Wisterias

Super8 film thru
Cracks in the kal-
eid-o-scopic lens
reel spin

    -ing

[Hesitantly

One. . .two. . .click
One. . .two. . .click

One. . .

Two. . .

I am fully aware,

humming]

Baroque lullabies
Bend to lip your eyes
Broken-drown shards
Drowning in the earth

THE STRAYING F[r]ICTION

...and yet we think the greatest pain's to die.
-John Keats

AND

Across this land we walked and talked, and talked and walked, until there was nothing more to walk or talk about. Even so, we continued to do our best because that's all we've ever known.

LOOK

Krista, can't you see it all so clearly now? There, there, the rain is gone and we should feel no more guilt. Are those fractured sunsets hiding underneath our bed? No. I've taken the liberty of cleaning unrealities. Some find it morbid, but others would die for dreams of nooses and bubble-blowing harmonicas.

LET'S

Invent a new philosophy and then hate ourselves for being so evilly pretentious, but if we were to pretend then let our philosophy be something that's more conservative; something true to basic fundamentals. Let's do this not to be political or religious per say, but rather because we have now come to the conclusion that Progression is a pretty lie.

LIE

Love, I know you want to record my swan song in my sleep, but you can't, not just yet. You see, I see some turnip sky peeping through a pinhole in a dusty portrait of Stalin; the painting that your great grandfather found on the roadside. Our very (young) lives revolve around walking and talking about the path, this path, this land; the sand, the sand, the sand, the...the...the.

NOTE: If we are to pretend that you have left the poem, 'you' will take the informal third-person.

LOOK UP

She studies those tree branches that once had a voice; trees that have been silenced by time.

SPEAK

Our love is a beautiful focus brewed ironically from straying f[r]iction. We associate ourselves with the quest for perfection and we walk and we talk and we talk and we talk; speaking of speaking, I must mention that nothing is so easy to come by these days as an equation to a make-believe family. With our eyes and mouths shut tightly let's not taste or see anymore of this path, this land, this sand, this...this...this...launch us...

UP

Her eyes are cream-pink the color of a dog's shaved undercarriage

(Before she died)

She must have made a pact with The Sun
& *the heat, the heat, the heat,*
The Sun bubbles-up her skin
Tapping her veins
Shriveled

(Earth's seasons care nothing for the dead)

We cross over hissing creaks
Shaped like slender snakes
Stepping onto steep banks
Where hands grab at my ankles

Broken out through the soil
Some flashing wedding rings
The clouds reflect the mountains ahead
She stinks of slaughtered pigs wrapped in shit

(Seven months, seven months, seven months)

NEW SMYRNA BEACH, FLORIDA

...and they're searching for the missing
[4] bottles of little pink pills.
Father paces barefoot in silence.
Mother speaks while Sister translates.
& I am lost to *The blur*
[Red] dimensions of infinity

CHARLOTTE, NORTH CAROLINA

@18 : New title : PanicKing
$240 = 12 tabs   of   -e-
bestowed upon   me
by the hands of the   Old
Char-**lotte[ry]** Coliseum
tax free   TAX   FREE
gnawed through my lip
Crusty-cum-stain-motel
floor **where I slept** on
D A Y S   I N N
before passing through
the light, 5 o'clock traffic-
jam I N D E P E N D E N C E
on the boulevard   I
saw a bum &   a cop
r   o   l   l   i   n   g
down the side- **walk**
with a hooker   screaming
daddy   baby   daddy
she had a raisin for a face
when **She opened up wide**
M   O   T   H   S
flew out of her mouth &
the walls of building **bent forward**
H A I L I N G   ME as their King
and It **was** that way **all the way**
into Mecklenburg **Count**y suburbs
where they **fed me** rai**sins** for free   *because*

"*Anima*, actualized"

Tonight is like your last night's view of my body from
behind
Curled-up and naked inside your open window pane
The sweat-shine on my skin reflecting the Technicolor
City's glow
As I savor the final burn from another *Gitane* with the filter
ripped off

You exhale the softest of laughs and gently finger
My shoulder's pool of blended light and by now
All of our awkwardness has since been addressed
With one long descriptive open-ended question
That's been patiently answered not once but twice

Earlier tonight I knew I had been turned into a shrimp
named Selí
Swimming against the strong currents of complex zigzag
patterns
And ricocheting off the high-pitch of crisscrossing echoes
But now that I'm lost in the layers of unfamiliar texture
Now that I'm lost in the absence of familiar physical
markers
I ask myself *is this not just another high-definition dream?*
Or *is this what it feels like to be marinated in*
Your sweet-ginger West Coast taste?

From below I hear echoes echoing more echoes
All these echoes are circling me from every angle
Like tiny callused newborn fingers raking over blue
Candy bars covered in Braille-print plastic
Wrapping scratches ascend to a deafening-white
Pitch that is gnawing through my flesh as I lay
On my back trying to gasp the deepest of breaths
While the crinkle-crackle-crackle cracklings bleat their
collective cry A thousand of candy wrappers explode in a
magnificent chemical red

As the sun melts the wax from my wings

I can hear Peter's voice, rattling
Between drags off a Marlboro Red.
And over the wind he says,

"My boy, everything comes
Full circle," and, "how you get
In is how you get out…"

I look down to see
Her face taking shape
In the white-cap sea. Two

Waves break on top of her, erasing
Her brown eyes and opening her mouth;
I can *almost* smell her breath.

INTERVAL
[A]

for paper planes disappeared long ago
my Hercules, were you ever there?
sounds claw my eardrums like fever

dolls melting on hotdog grills
and Labor Day lynching
silent picture shows

where human bones
hold flavor
open

e
y
e

found time
dead to sound
inadequate

my experiment
elapsed in the crevice
all of the evils between

Pluto's two thighs are a daydream
pick me up at the magazine hut
if I told her, she wouldn't believe me

see your pencil rolling off the desk
having its way with gravity
suspended in cream-burst air

an act that defies all
laws of reasoning
mother: a pear

alone to
bridge
the stars

INTERVAL
[B]

& what could be said of the man with exotic fish for hands?
& what could be said of the woman who drew veins in the
sky?
& what could be said of the boy who turned the hunt on
himself?

I saw that man once, the one with the exotic fish for hands!
I saw that woman once, the one who drew veins in the sky!
I saw that boy once, the one who turned the hunt on
himself!

Then tell us what could be said of this man???
Then tell us what could be said of this woman???
Then tell us what could be said of this boy???

INTERVAL
[C]

Lost in your reflection coming off rainbow-stained oil
puddles
Lost in the jelly eggs floating in a plastic container of tapioca
Lost in calculating the morning's grey ocean tides

Lost in pointing to storm clouds clotting the veins of a red
horizon
Lost in the sounds rising from your neighbor's basement
Lost in videotaping your life through red filters: memories:
blue

Lost in using a calculator to measure the patterns of the
winds
Lost in beckoning sharks at sunset with the shimmer of a
fake Rolex
Lost in measuring the infinite blurring of time and echoes:
listen

Lost in the anxiety of your date sharpening her chopsticks
Lost in finding timeless comfort in broken bedside clocks
Lost in fucking women who remind you of people you
despise

Lost in expecting cats to act like birds
Lost in forgetting poetry to dissect fish
Lost in skinning fish skin to save the silver scales

Lost in cutting pedestrian paths through infected jungles
Lost in tossing peanut shells to dead elephants behind bars
Lost in a cough

Lost in the found drawer to regret the original loss now
found
Lost in attempting to breed with an apathetic Sun
Lost in failing to spin the Yo-Yo

Lost in the giant's stalemate
Lost in envying the eagerness of a dying man
Lost in false identities masked with somewhat partial truths

Lost in drug rehab centers to be found in university rooms
Lost in the distance between the X and Y
Lost in proper package tracking

Lost in an invisible sickness as if they never cared to save
you
Lost in the eyes of a dying squirrel
Lost in gunshots that ring about the china room

When the answers fail to show

I watch you
Mumbling
Picking bugs off your face
They come from the lava flow(s)
I don't see
The bugs not the bugs but
Sulfuric stench setting in
Shattered glass parking lot
Ants burrowing
Yellow-brick road burning
Into your eyelids swollen
Amputated lash *(s)* singed
Infections of the shy kind
That invisible…

My Serenity's
©

ther eisap atter
nfor min gwith
jete ngin esst atic
-blurf orm ati
onofga sses so
meov ereas yeg
gsand di
scon tent

he arethes oldier
svoice slikecan
nonb allsrin
ging myste
rybell sof
noca bleout

letthem
fallo utint
oth eRE-AL
la titud inalper
sua sion ofa
numb erings
yst emcreat
edfr omnot
hing

Stepping Through a Jet-Low

Say goodbye to the unborn, and push
the Boat of the Dead to sea. Pray
as your watch it catch flame,
a small torch on the horizon.

The Visitor

Black iron bars over the windows
Create grids slicing small squares
Into the palm trees and blue skies
Just outside of this psyche hospital
Reminding me of all those scattered
Pieces of the tropical-themed jigsaw
That   *we* could never fully connect.

So Memory Says,

THE MAN REMEMBERS

THE EXACT MOMENT AFTER

HIS 'OLD BEING' WAS

INTRODUCED TO A 'NEW'

There were thousands of trees, endless rows of black
Trees that resembled enormous hypodermic needles
Standing upright, aimed toward Heaven, and poised
To empty their swollen syringes of dried-out Thorazine
Over the gutted path of burnt grass; blackened blades
That crackled sharply beneath the man's red-blistered feet
When he took off running to touch the bark of the trees,
And when he rubbed his hands over the faces of the trees
They all dissolved, and collapsed instantly—wayward clouds
Of ash, cascading through his frail spread fingers...

THEN HE REMEMBERS BEING

JARRED AWAKE BY THE MANIC

WAILINGS OF PATIENTS,

HIS PEERS; STRANGERS

VOICES MELDING INTO

ONE, UNANSWERED ECHO

My plan

for when I be———————come

                    alive
                    again,
I want
to forget

                         every-
                         thing

        I had to
        remember

            just
            before
             I

                    died
                     the last time.

THE BOYS

grimaced when walking straight lines,

wobbled at the concept of unborn forms,

explored gray spaces to reveal things,

barked like dogs running from their owners' warrants,

disrespected all manipulated ideas of Sleep,

left the pregnant sow still and bloodied in the yard,

wished to snap the last branch of the family tree,

and reasoned not to have any more rational reasons.

THE BEATINGS WITHIN

Rising out of the metallic ringing, the old woman realized that her grandsons' shotgun shrapnel had scattered high overhead *She had not died*. When she put an ear to her husband's chest, she was immediately reminded of those bright mornings when they would wake, limb-wrapped, in vast fields of ice and snow. Grinning on this memory, the old woman expected to hear the sweet sounds of frozen earth separating under her sole; but, instead she heard thousands of babies screaming hysterically.

UN-repair-ABLE damage

Perhaps we should just pack up our feelings and head home, because maybe the end has already come to pass. Yet, it's the absences that send me searching for fillers. It's about the holes that he bore into my body and mind; it's about the holes that he will probably never repair. *You see, I am porous. You see, I drain.* Horrified and exhausted, his fingers fled on nails long ago, before his eyes could witness the destruction. The man exists, under covers, to dream of red horizons filled with nude Examples.

TRANSITIONS

His heart hiccups as the engines of the airplane start. The prickled ringing in his ears deepens into a stout, purring bass. As for leaving the comforts of the factory and the only Experience he's ever known? Well, it's not a natural thing. He understands there is no turning back, and he can sense that his fate might be sealed to the act of leaving.

As the plane starts to speed, his ears pop and his eyes open just in time to see the plane blazing through the soot-smeared mouth of the smokestack. He is lifted up into the sky. Terrified by the rattling of the wings cutting through the foreign air, he hums loudly to block the sound out. He also considers how difficult it will be, adjusting to the pure-bright glare of the sun and clouds. Thousands of feet below, in a hole, his life is a collection of ash.

RUINS

Once through the backdoor of
the Mansion of Sleep, they took
a fantastic leap from the marble threshold
and closed their eyes. There were
                    colorful variations:

                    Nebraska,
         Nebraska,   Nebraska,
                    Nebraska.

They landed
in the middle of a wheat field.
                    Bir-thing.
                    Eyes wide open.
              A path snaked through
all that endless wheat, dividing
the red-rust stalks like opposing river banks.

Now...
if with your own eyes,
you were to follow the path all the way,
then you'd see how it went into the jaws of the woods.
Well, they saw, and, in an instant, they knew...

Those woods were *the* reason why
they had fled The Mansion. Slip.
There they would search for all that
Sleep had stolen from them.

It was hot.
There was an invisible decay.
There were flies and
There were unanswered questions.
They trudged the sticky-
pink, twisting trail.

Over-

head
high-
chirps and guttural echoes
competed for the loudest echo.

Beneath
them
fallen tree branches
seemed to stretch on forever
and across the ancient roots of trees;
trees that were once looming
powers, but were now
incomplete amputees.

It was then, in the woods,
they heard *them*—our abducted dreams—
calling them by their first names
from within
the branches at our feet.

But, as they reached down
to snap and release them from the bark,
they noticed the moonlight fading.
There were no more
shadows stretched across the forest floor.

They looked up to see
the moon being eclipsed by a creeping
canvas of blackbirds flapping across the sky.
Their direction was lost.
More questions:
Deseret,
Deseret,
Deseret,
Deseret
        whispering…

As they were sucked into the vortex of darkness—
while overhead noises overwhelmed The Dream Talk
and the birds smothered the moonlight—they realized that

they had nothing to show that they'd gotten the better of Sleep.

Skip.
Breathe.
Skip. Bend-
over. Be nauseous.
There was nothing
to prove they had ever existed
outside of The Mansion.

Unreachable Planes

After a spice or two from the sand dunes, pleasant dreams slide
Down into a world of nightmares: the ocean stands up, taking
The shape of a giant serpent's tongue, coming to suck me off
My parent's balcony where, curled like a cooked shrimp,
I hide underneath my father's favorite rocking chair;
Occasionally peering through slits in the wickerweave
To witness the big black clumsy, licking the sun's secret organ.
And that is when I come to believe– my father's rocking chair is
The only thing, on this Earth, that can shelter me from what's to
come.

What Kills You
-riffing on Blas de Otero's "Lo Fatal"

Surrounded by illnesses and catastrophes
surrounded by cloudy towers and mist
this is how I see you
my defenseless dove
surrounded by boats with half-closed eyelids
surrounded by snow and lightning
with your doll-like wrists and thighs
surrounded by councils and pharmacies
your forehead burns my lips from kissing
with a handkerchief smothering your voice
with your womb of transparent host
surrounded by corners and depressing announcements
surrounded by bishops
with your pale poppy knees
this is how I found you and see you
surrounded by all the catastrophes and schools
gripping the outer edge of your soul with your finger of smoke
accompanying my honorable disasters
defenseless dove
youth riding from branch to branch
between boats and desolate docks
last youth of the world
telegram stamped by the dawn
by the centuries of the centuries
in this way I see you in this way I find you
and I lose nights fallen over barbed wire fences
planes palpitate in the radar of your heart
blue bell of the sky
glorious sunset before evening's desolation
giving way to the crowds
as a bright star amongst crystal windows
surrounded by illnesses and catastrophes
this is how I find you on the brink of death
dressed in violet and bird glimpsed
preoccupied with your ragged foot
descending the steps of my poetry

Notes & Acknowledgments

Theology of the Body

Quotes between poems were adapted from the following sources:

Jason Evert,
The Pontifical Council of the Family,
Pope John Paul II,
Proverbs,
St. Paul, &
Christopher West.

The majority of these poems were initially published in slightly altered forms by *27 rue de fleures*, *Baltimore Is Reads*, Blood Pudding Press, dancing girl press, *blossombones*, *Chantarelle's Notebook* (Online and Print Editions), *Conte*, *DOGZPLOT*, *Eight Octaves Review*, *elimae*, Gold Wake Press, *The Harrow*, Maverick Duck Press, *NANO Fiction*, *Night Train*, *The Orange Room Review*, *The Real Eight View*, *Sawbuck*, *Segue*, *Sein und Werden*, *Spork*, *Wheelhouse Magazine*, *Willows Wept Review*, and *Word Riot*.

"Ruin" was also nominated for *Best of the Net*. Special thanks to Robert P. Arthur, Christine Gelineau, J. Michael Wahlgren and Sean Kilpatrick.

The Silence of Sickness

Some of these poems were previously published by *Common-Line*, *Counterexample Poetics*, Gold Wake Press, Kendra Steiner Editions, *Mud Luscious*, Pudding House Publications, Scintillating Publications, and *Underground Voices*

Donora Hillard has published with BlazeVox [books], dancing girl press, Gold Wake Press, and others. Her creative nonfiction, fiction, photography, and poetry have appeared or are forthcoming in *Night Train*, *The Norton Anthology of Hint Fiction*, *Pebble Lake Review*, *Segue*, and elsewhere. She has taught writing at Penn State University and lives in Detroit, Michigan, where she is a PhD candidate in English at Wayne State University.

Zachary C. Bush is the author of three books of poetry: 'Angles of Disorder' (BlazeVOX books, 2010), 'At Swan Decapitation' (VOX Press, 2011) and 'Silence of Sickness' (Gold Wake Press, 2011). He holds a B.A. in Writing and Linguistics from Georgia Southern University, a M.F.A. in Poetry from the City College of New York, and is a doctoral candidate of Mythological Literature at Drew University. In the fall of 2012, Bush will begin M.A. studies in Theology at the Union Theological Seminary (NYC). Bush teaches English at Berkeley College (NYC), Pace University and Kean University. He and his fiancee live in Hoboken, NJ.

CPSIA information can be obtained at www.ICGtesting.com
Printed in the USA
BVOW031741300512

291386BV00001B/21/P